OTABIND

Dear Friend:

You may have noticed that this book is put together differently than most other quality paperbacks. The page you are reading, for instance, along with the back page, is glued to the cover. And when you open the book the spine "floats" in back of the pages. But there's nothing wrong with your book. These features allow us to produce what is known as a detached cover, specifically designed to prevent the spine from cracking even after repeated use. A state-of-the-art binding technology known as OtaBind® is used in the manufacturing of this and all Health Communications, Inc. books.

HCI has invested in equipment and resources that ensure the books we produce are of the highest quality, yet remain affordable. At our Deerfield Beach headquarters, our editorial and art departments are just a few steps from our pressroom, bindery and shipping facilities. This internal production enables us to pay special attention to the needs of our readers when we create our books.

Our titles are written to help you improve the quality of your life. You may find yourself referring to this book repeatedly, and you may want to share it with family and friends who can also benefit from the information it contains. For these reasons, our books have to be durable and, more importantly, user-friendly.

OtaBind® gives us these qualities. Along with a crease-free spine, the book you have in your hands has some other characteristics you may not be aware of:

- Open the book to any page and it will lie flat, so you'll never have to worry about losing your place.

- You can bend the book over backwards without damage, allowing you to hold it with one hand.

- The spine is 3-5 times stronger than conventional perfect binding, preventing damage even with rough handling.

This all adds up to a better product for our readers—one that will last for years to come. We stand behind the quality of our books and guarantee that, if you're not completely satisfied, we'll replace the book or refund your money within 30 days of purchase. If you have any questions about this guarantee or our bookbinding process, please feel free to contact our customer service department at 1-800-851-9100.

We hope you enjoy the quality of this book, and find understanding, insight and direction for your life in the information it provides.

Health Communications, Inc.®
3201 S.W. 15th Street
Deerfield Beach, FL 33442-8190
(305) 360-0909

Peter Vegso
President

KINDLING THE SPIRIT

*K*indling THE SPIRIT

Acts of Kindness and Words of Courage for Women

*L*ois P. *F*rankel, Ph.D.

Health Communications, Inc.
Deerfield Beach, Florida

©1994 Lois P. Frankel
ISBN 1-55874-323-5

Publisher: Health Communications, Inc.
            3201 S.W. 15th Street
            Deerfield Beach, Florida 33442-8190

Cover Design By Robert Cannata

This book is dedicated to women everywhere
who have time for everyone except themselves
with the hope that we may begin showing
ourselves the same kindnesses we do others
and to Shirley and Joyce — who taught me
the real meaning of self-kindness.

$\mathcal{I}$NTRODUCTION

In my last book, *Women, Anger and Depression*, I explored the concept of how women's unexpressed anger relates to depression. Chapter Seven, "The Ten Commandments of Taking Charge of Your Life," listed ways of taking back the control and power that women so frequently give to others. The Sixth Commandment, Thou Shalt Feed Thyself as Well as Others, generated many questions from readers. Women who took the time to call and write knew that they should do this, but wanted to know how. I wanted to know why women couldn't see ways in which they could nurture themselves.

Anna Freud said, "It is the good, capable, conscientious woman who is more likely to be depressed than her counterparts." Paradoxically, the woman who does so much for others creates her own depression and has little energy left to spend on herself! As women, we have no role models to follow for taking care of ourselves as well as we do others. In my readings I recall a line from a book (and for the life of me I can't remember which one) that said "women are the caretakers, nurturers and accommodators" in society. Actually, we have learned this role so well that when we think about feeding ourselves we experience feelings of guilt, shame or selfishness.

I had thought about the dilemma for nearly a year when the answer suddenly became clear at the oddest moment. It had been a particularly busy time for me and, while chopping vegetables for a dinner party, I thought to myself, "I wish I had just a little bit of time for myself." This led to other questions such as "What would I do if I did have the time?" and "Why don't I take more time for myself?" and "What's the worst thing that would happen if I took time to do something I really enjoy?" I vowed at that moment to take a little time each day just for me.

The seconds following the vow were filled with thoughts that I realized had less to do with me than with society's messages I had internalized. I began thinking that I didn't have enough time for family and friends, so how could I even think about doing something nice for myself during the course of each day? I worried that my work would suffer. I had worked hard to build an international consulting business and it could all go down the drain if I acted self-indulgently. I worried that people would see me as selfish. I also knew that if I felt this way while doing workshops that encourage women to take better care of themselves, then certainly other women did, too.

As I continued to think about it, I realized that an act of self-kindness didn't have to take a lot of time or cost any money. It only had to be a few minutes carved out of each day that was mine alone; a time that I could give myself permission to use as I saw fit and to replenish the well that is often left dry by doing for others.

While writing *Kindling the Spirit* I spoke with friends about the concept for this book, and quite naturally they each began generating what they perceived to be acts of self-kindness that could be included. It was surprising how many times their first ideas were to "tell someone else something that you like about them" or "do a good deed for someone." When I suggested that this wasn't an act of self-kindness but rather an act of kindness to and for another, they invariably disagreed. They believed that doing something nice for someone else made oneself feel good. And herein lies the issue: Our good feelings about ourselves are all too often related to the act of doing for others. Our self-worth and self-concept are *other*-oriented, rather than *inner*-oriented. So much of our satisfaction comes from the deeds we do for others, not the deeds that we do for ourselves.

Taking this one step further, there are many times we think we are doing something nice for ourselves when we are actually engaging in self-punishment and/or other-oriented behavior. The time spent at the hairdresser having our hair colored or the hours spent on the stationary bicycle or even the week spent at a health spa aren't really acts of self-kindness. They make us feel better about being women in a society that expects impeccable grooming and svelte figures, and we have come to believe that they are for us. However, eating a banana split without feeling guilty or worrying about the calories is a true act of self-kindness!

As readers of my last book know, I'm a firm believer in "be careful of what you wish for because you're going to get it." Self-kindness follows this maxim. The more you focus on self-kindness, the more naturally it comes. If you are kind to yourself, fairly soon you will expect no less from those around you.

I hope that you will find, as I have, that self-kindness isn't as difficult as it may initially seem. Self-kindness is born of the desire for self-preservation in a world that takes so much away from women. The analogy I use when working with women is that of the old-fashioned well from which water used to be retrieved. You could dip into it many times but eventually the well would become dry if it wasn't replenished. The analogy that Mother Teresa uses is, "To keep a lamp burning we have to keep putting oil in it."

Women's wells run dry and candles burn out by the constant drain of time, energy and resources spent on others. We must take responsibility for replenishing our own spirits if we are to be able to survive in a healthy way. We must take time for ourselves if we are to continue feeding others. We must feed our own spirits if we are to have any hope of nourishing anyone else's.

Kindling the Spirit is written for those who are so caught up in their other-orientation, or so consumed with guilty feelings when they do something nice for themselves, that they can't even think of what to do for themselves because of the feelings associated with self-kindness. It's designed to get you into the habit of thinking about yourself and your needs for at least some portion of each day. Doing something that's just for you . . . no one else. This is why I haven't included acts related to exercise, grooming or charitable volunteer work, although it's true that they can make you feel better about yourself, because they're hard work and often other-oriented. The activities included were ones I felt were reasonable, in terms of cost and the time spent. For each activity there is an accompanying quotation by a woman, well known or otherwise, to serve as an inspiration on your path toward self-kindness.

As I researched the writings of women for quotations, I found that their insight and the power of their words kindled my own spirit. My writing always begins with the desire to help others and results in my being helped as much as I hope the reader is. *Kindling the Spirit* is no different. I found myself taking more time to actually engage in the activities I suggested in this book, and thinking more about what I could do for myself that would replenish my well. I can't say that anyone would say, "Oh, hasn't Lois changed," for either good or bad. I only know that now when I come home late at night I look up into the sky and search for the star that I've claimed as my own and, combined with my other acts of self-kindness, I refresh my spirit and better enable myself to handle the many challenges that life brings.

The goal isn't for you to engage in every act of kindness included in the book. As a matter of fact, there may only be a dozen or so that you would really enjoy. Just because an act is written here doesn't mean you must do it. A large part of self-kindness involves giving yourself permission to not do things that you think you should or must. Begin by choosing those acts that are most appealing to you and that are easy for you to engage in. Don't set yourself up to fail. For example, it wouldn't be appropriate to choose the act of taking the afternoon off to do something you've been wanting to do for a long time but thought was frivolous when your boss has scheduled a meeting with the company brass!

Perhaps a letter that I recently received from a woman in one of my workshops best expresses the concept of giving yourself permission to engage in acts of self-kindness:

> *Ever since returning from your "Women in Charge" program it's been on my mind to write, say thank you and ask if others often comment on "what a difference a day makes." As I drove home I realized that I had a sense of well-being I hadn't had in a long time—and wondered if it would be with me the next morning. At the market there was a beautiful tuberose and I bought it—just for myself. The next day I was shopping for a birthday gift. I found something that I thought was just right and also saw something I really liked for myself. I bought both, the first time in decades I had bought a piece of jewelry for myself. Lest you think I am squandering my grandchildren's inheritance, let me say that this was quite enough and these small pleasures represent a permission I had been unwilling to give myself—and now have.*

Once you've gotten used to the idea of treating yourself with kindness, such as the author of this letter, select two or three acts from this book that you originally skipped over because you thought you'd never have the time for them or that they seemed too self-indulgent. You'll find that the more you treat yourself with kindness the easier it becomes on a regular basis. Most people will never even notice you're doing anything differently. Soon you won't need this book to find ideas for your own acts for *Kindling the Spirit*.

Dr. Lois P. Frankel

Resolve to engage in one act of self-kindness each and every day of the year.

If women were convinced that a day off or an hour of solitude was a reasonable ambition, they would find a way of attaining it. As it is, they feel so unjustified in their demand that they rarely make the attempt.

Anne Morrow Lindbergh
A Gift from the Sea

Make a cup of tea or hot cocoa and drink it while it's still hot, savoring the warm feeling as it flows through your body.

Tea to the English is really a picnic indoors.

Alice Walker
The Color Purple

Break out of the boundaries that have been circumscribed for you through birth, race, gender or age, and forge your own path.

Do not follow where the path may lead. Go instead where there is no path and leave a trail.

Muriel Strode

Visit a museum, paying particular attention to the early women artists who overcame tremendous odds to be allowed to express their creativity.

Achievement in the arts and humanities is reserved now, as it has been historically, for males. Token representation . . . does not vitiate this rule.

Kate Millet
Sexual Politics

Visit with a friend and share the warmth that can only pass between two people who care deeply for one another.

[For women], the center of the universe is relationships. Everything else must go through, relate to, and be defined by relationships.

Anne Wilson Schaef
Women's Reality

Watch a travelogue about a far away place that you've only dreamed of visiting and plan for the time when you will.

Through travel I first became aware of the outside world; it was through travel that I found my own introspective way into becoming a part of it.

Eudora Welty
One Writer's Beginnings

*A*sk someone for something that you need and accept the gift with grace.

Besides giving ourselves what we need, begin to ask people for what we need and want from them because this is part of taking care of ourselves and being a responsible human being.

Melody Beattie
Co-dependent No More

$\mathcal{P}$ut something off until tomorrow with the knowledge that it will still be waiting for you and the world won't end as a result.

I'll think of that tomorrow . . . After all, tomorrow is another day.

Scarlett O'Hara
Gone with the Wind

Make a list of your best characteristics, stop only when you have reached at least fifty, then post it where you can read it throughout the day.

Character cannot be developed in ease and quiet. Only through experience of trial and suffering can the soul be strengthened, vision cleared, ambition inspired and success achieved.

Helen Keller
Helen Keller's Journal

Pick or buy a flower, place it prominently in your home and experience the wonder of nature's beauty each time you look at it.

When you take a flower in your hand and really look at it, it's your world for the moment.

Georgia O'Keeffe

10

Take a hot bath and feel the relaxation that comes from immersing yourself in something other than the day's problems.

There must be quite a few things that a hot bath won't cure, but I don't know many of them.

Sylvia Plath
The Bell Jar

*F*orgive yourself for a past mistake — allow yourself to be human in a world that too often demands perfection.

No one can make you feel inferior without your consent.

Eleanor Roosevelt

Take a walk in the rain on a summer day
allowing your skin to drink in the droplets
of moisture in much the same way
as a flower might.

Surround of rainbows
Listen
The rain comes upon us
Restore us.

Meridel Le Sueur
Rites of Ancient Ripening

Plan a regular night out with other women who share your interests . . . and don't permit anyone else's last minute needs or plans to cancel yours.

And I was to find out then, as I found out many times over and over again, that women are not content with just a husband and family, but must have a community, a group, an exchange with others . . . Young and old, even in the busiest years of our lives, we women especially are victims of the long loneliness.

Dorothy Day
The Long Loneliness

$\mathscr{F}$ind a serene, comfortable spot—be it a couch, park, chair or beach—to take a nap in the middle of the afternoon.

$\mathscr{A}$s we get older we must increasingly worry about conserving energy ... caring for our bodies and our minds instead of spending them carelessly.

Mary Catherine Bateson
Composing a Life

15

Tell someone what you *really* think instead of what you think they want to hear.

But now I know the things I know; And do the things I do; And if you do not like me so, To hell, my love, with you!

Dorothy Parker
Indian Summer

Leave the bed unmade today . . .

Housekeeping ain't no joke.

Louisa May Alcott
Little Women

. . . And the dirty dishes in the sink overnight.

Housework is the hardest work in the world. That's why men don't do it.

Edna Ferber
So Big

Don't take "I'm sorry, there's nothing I can do," for an answer because there is . . .

As soon as many women think of incurring some-one else's displeasure—especially a man's—they equate it with abandonment. . . . If women avoid taking this risk, in most cases they cannot begin the journey.

Dr. Jean Baker Miller
Toward a New Psychology of Women

Whistle as loud as you can for as long as you like.

I was told that whistling wasn't ladylike, but I knew even then that women were simply not supposed to be that happy.

Anonymous

$\mathcal{D}$raw a picture with crayons of the place where you had your happiest moment without judging your work as good or bad . . . just remembering the moment.

$\mathcal{D}$rawing enables you to see in that special, epiphanous way. Your goal in drawing should be to encounter the reality of experience—to see ever more clearly, ever more deeply.

Betty Edwards
Drawing on the Right Side of the Brain

Meditate for fifteen minutes allowing your mind to wander toward those thoughts that are your greatest source of contentment.

There are no evil thoughts except one: the refusal to think.

Ayn Rand
Atlas Shrugged

Watch the puppies in a pet store window.

I think dogs are the most amazing creatures; they give unconditional love. This makes them my role model for being alive.

Gilda Radner

Turn off the answering machine and unplug the phone to create a silent space free from the intrusion of others.

As a teenager you are at the last stage in your life when you will be happy to hear that the phone is for you.

Fran Lebowitz
Social Studies

Write a letter to someone you really care about but never seem to find the time to correspond with except during the holidays.

A letter always seemed to me like immortality because it is the mind alone without corporeal friend.

Emily Dickinson

Go outside tonight, look at the stars and claim
one to be yours forever and yours alone.

*When we are chafed and fretted by small cares, a
look at the stars will show us the littleness of our
own interests.*

Maria Mitchell
Life, Letters and Journals

For once, allow yourself to cry without knowing exactly why and without saying, "I really have nothing to cry about . . . there are so many people a lot worse off than me."

Those who do not know how to weep with their whole heart don't know how to laugh either.

Golda Meir

Challenge the way that your mother did it . . .
do it your own way.

Protocol is not there to dictate to you. It's there to help you. You have to have the courage and security to do it your way.

Barbara Bush

Do the one thing that you've been told is impossible to do and feel the triumph that comes from overcoming the fear of others.

I was a slave in the state of New York and now I am a good citizen coming forth to speak about women's rights. We have all been thrown down so low that nobody thought we'd ever get up again— but we have been long enough trodden—now we will come up again.

Sojourner Truth

Enroll in a degree program, class or
workshop that will give you the skills,
knowledge or credentials needed to
increase your self-confidence.

*But I think that education, and only education, has
saved, and can continue to save, American women
from the greater dangers of the feminine mystique.*

Betty Friedan
The Feminine Mystique

Embrace your femininity by prohibiting anyone to label you with it.

To be somebody, a woman does not have to be more like a man, but has to be more of a woman.

Sally E. Shaywitz

Make your voice heard by standing up for
something you believe in.

*Cautious, careful people, always casting about to
preserve their reputations . . . can never effect reform.*

Susan B. Anthony

Go outside just before sunset and
watch the sky alight with color
as it bids another day good-bye.

Each night the sunset surged with purple pampas-
grass plumes, and shot fuchsia rockets into the pink
sky, then deepened through folded layers of peacock
green to all the blues of India and a black across
which clouds sometimes churned alabaster dolls.

Diane Ackerman
A Natural History of the Senses

ℬe the leader today . . . whether it's to lead a discussion, a group of hikers or a team of people to a new and exciting place.

Do not wait for leaders; do it alone, person to person.

Mother Teresa

$\mathcal{R}$e-open a door that was once closed to you by saying to yourself "I deserve better."

You may have to fight a battle more than once to win it.

Margaret Thatcher

Brag about your accomplishments—let others know how proud you are of *you*.

Broadway has been very good to me; but then I've been very good to Broadway.

Ethel Merman

Allow your anger to emerge, directed toward the person or thing to which it belongs instead of toward yourself.

Anger is a signal, and one worth listening to.

Harriet Lerner
The Dance of Anger

Challenge the status quo by asking "Why?" and refusing to accept "Because that's the way things are" for an answer.

We are not afraid to rock the boat. Making waves. That is what Asian American women have done and will continue to do.

Asian Women United of California

Go to the library and check out a book
about a woman who has changed
the course of history.

*I have crossed over the backs of Sojourner Truth,
Harriet Tubman, Fannie Lou Hamer and Madam
C. J. Walker. Because of them I can now live the
dream. I am the seed of the free and I know it. I
intend to bear great fruit.*

Oprah Winfrey

Spend a half hour lost in your dreams.

*Women have never had a half hour in all their lives
(except before or after anybody is up in the house)
that they can call their own, without fear of offend-
ing or hurting someone.*

Florence Nightingale

From the recesses of your memory, call upon a fond moment with someone from your past.

Gentle ladies, you will remember till old age what we did together in our brilliant youth.

Sappho

Stay home alone while everyone else goes out for the evening and, if nothing else, listen to the sound of the clock ticking.

One lives and endures one's life with others, within matrices, but it is only alone, truly alone, that one bursts apart, springs forth.

**Maria Isabel Barreno,
Maria Fatima Velho da Costa and
Maria Teresa Horta**
New Portuguese Letters

$\mathcal{L}$et others see your brilliance instead of hiding it for fear of outshining them.

As things are, women are ill-used. They are forced to live a life of imbecility, and are blamed for doing so.

George Sand
La Fauvette du Docteur

$\mathcal{L}$earn about something that piques your interest and is entirely novel—and useless—to you.

For human beings are not so constituted that they cannot live without expansion; and if they do not get it one way, [they] must another, or perish.

Margaret Fuller

Surround yourself with lit candles in a dark room and be lost in the warm glow and dancing shadows they create.

There are two ways of spreading light: to be the candle or the mirror that receives it.

Edith Wharton
Vesalius in Zante

Move your body freely to the rhythms of gentle music, listening carefully to the message you create.

The dance is a poem of which every movement is a word.

Mata Hari

Do something that would make others say,
"That's so out of character for her!"

You were once wild here. Don't let them tame you.

Isadora Duncan

Make a silent promise to take your soul to where it longs to be.

The vows one makes privately are more binding than any ceremony.

Beatrice Lilly

$\mathcal{L}$et go of whatever you've been pretending about for so long that it has obscured the essence of who you are.

When one is pretending, the entire body revolts.

Anaïs Nin

Spend an entire unplanned day alone doing whatever captures your interest at the moment.

I never said, "I want to be alone." I only said, "I want to be left alone." There is all the difference.

Greta Garbo

Make one list of all the things you like about your life and a second about the things you dislike. Then make a third list . . . what you're going to do about the second.

Risk! Risk anything! Care no more for the opinions of others, for those voices. Do the hardest thing on earth for you. Act for yourself. Face the truth.

Katherine Mansfield

Do the one thing that you would regret never having done if your life ended tomorrow.

I have always spoken my mind . . . followed my desires and impulses . . . so that I have no need to get even with my past now.

Simone de Beauvoir
After the Second Sex

Choose a sport that would be fun for you and play it without thought of how good you are.

I have never thought of participating in a sport just for the sake of doing it for exercise or as a means of losing weight. I really enjoy playing it. It's a vital part of my life.

Dinah Shore

$\mathcal{B}$e first: whether it's to choose the best seat at the movies, the first to give an opinion or the first to drink the last of the milk.

In an elitist world, it's always been "women and children last."

Marge Piercy
Sisterhood Is Powerful

$\mathcal{P}$lan an adventure that will free your spirit to soar wildly and unashamedly.

Adventure is worthwhile in itself.

Amelia Earhart

Do something your own way instead of the way everyone else wants you to do it.

You've got to take the initiative to play your own game ... confidence makes the difference.

Chris Evert

Spoil yourself: for once take your cotton
blouses to the cleaners to be done for you.

You can't get spoiled if you do your own ironing.

Meryl Streep

Give yourself permission to appreciate where you currently are instead of where you think you should be.

Remember, no matter where you go, there you are.

Mary Engelbreit

Spend ten dollars at the dollar store on ten
different things that delight you.

*It's a grand thing to be able to take up your money
in hand and to think no more of it when it slips
away from you than you would a trout that would
slip back into the stream.*

Lady Gregory
Twenty Five

Take a drive into the country, stopping along
the way to notice the color of the sky, the
shapes of the trees and the sounds of the birds
as they try to speak to you.

*Those who dwell among the beauties and mysteries
of the earth are never weary of life . . . Those who
contemplate the beauty of the earth find reserves of
strength that will endure as long as life lasts.*

Rachael Carson
The Sense of Wonder

Go to your favorite restaurant with someone special, order your favorite food and savor every morsel and moment as your strength and your spirit are nourished.

Eating is not merely a material pleasure. Eating well gives a spectacular joy to life and contributes immensely to goodwill and happy companionship. It is of great importance to the morale.

Elsa Schiaparelli

Get the rest that you've been needing and wanting for so long, but haven't taken because you were afraid you'd be called "lazy."

My only concern was to get home after a hard day's work.

Rosa Parks

*V*isit a church, synagogue, mosque or other
spiritual dwelling and listen to the message
your internal spirit whispers when freed from
life's interruptions.

*We are not human beings trying to be spiritual, we
are spiritual beings trying to be human.*

Jacquelyn Small

Take a walk in the woods and breathe in the rich scent of the pines, oaks or cedars as they hover over and protect your path.

When I stepped away from the white pine, I had the definite feeling that we had exchanged some form of life energy . . . clearly white pines and I are on the same wavelength.

Anne Labastille
Woodswoman

Open a bank account that's yours alone and deposit whatever amount you can afford on a weekly basis so that you might have some financial security.

I've always been independent and I don't see how it conflicts with femininity.

Sylvia Porter

Roar at someone who deserves it.

It's better to be a lion for a day than a sheep all your life.

Sister Elizabeth Kenny

$\mathcal{B}$e spontaneous—allow yourself to say what you think, when you think it without worrying about how others might react.

What did she say? Just what she ought, of course. A lady always does.

Jane Austen

Bring a chair to the beach, a lake, river or stream and spend an hour listening to the rhythm of the water as it laps gently against the shore.

The voice of the sea speaks to the soul. The touch of the sea is sensuous, enfolding the body in its soft, close embrace.

Kate Chopin
The Awakening

Visit a candy store, buy one piece
of your very favorite chocolate and eat it
slowly while enjoying its delicious taste
as it melts in your mouth.

*Any month whose name contains the letter a, e or u
is the proper time for chocolate.*

Sandra Boynton,
Chocolate: The Consuming Passion

$\mathcal{D}$aydream about how you would like your life to be and envision ways of making it happen.

It seems to me that we can never give up longing and wishing while we are thoroughly alive. There are certain things we feel to be beautiful and good, and we must hunger after them.

George Eliot

$\mathcal{B}$egin a journal to record your dreams and
search the themes for meaning.

*Dreams say what they mean, but they don't say it
in daytime language.*

Gail Godwin
Dream Children

Read a novel, losing yourself in the people and places described.

Fiction reveals truth that reality obscures.

Jessamyn West

$\mathcal{L}$isten to Pachelbel's Canon from
beginning to end.

*Oh yes! The ascending from out of unconscious life
into revelation—that is music!*

Bettina von Arnim

Do one thing to simplify your life.

There are, in fact, certain roads that one may follow. Simplification of life is one of them.

Anne Morrow Lindbergh
A Gift from the Sea

$\mathcal{F}$ly a kite, watching it bob with freedom
as it rides on the wind.

Imagination is the highest kite one can fly.

Lauren Bacall

*H*ear the message your inner voice has for you if you will only trust yourself enough to listen.

Within all of us there is an inner voice ... if it's been covered over or if you are not practiced at listening to it, it may be very small ... yet it is there.

Ellen Bass and Laura Davis
The Courage to Heal

$\mathcal{U}$se your creativity: paint a picture, throw a
pot or write a poem, but create!

*Creative minds always have been known to survive
any kind of bad training.*

Anna Freud

*T*ell a white lie in answer to a question that shouldn't have been asked in the first place.

Never to lie is to have no lock to your door.

Elizabeth Bowen
The House in Paris

Break the rules: do something that you're not supposed to be able to do because you're a woman or you're black or you're differently abled or lacking formal education.

It is not easy to be a pioneer—but oh, it is fascinating! I would not trade one moment, even the worst moment, for all the riches in the world.

Elizabeth Blackwell

$\mathcal{F}$or just one day, forget about tomorrow
so that you may fully experience today.

*Love the moment, and the energy of that moment
will spread beyond all boundaries.*

Corita Kent

Tell a houseguest how long he or she is welcome to stay rather than waiting to be told how long the stay will last.

Superior people never make long visits.

Marianne Moore

Write a letter to an elected official letting him or her know how you feel about an issue impacting you.

It was we, the people; not we, the white male citizens; nor yet we, the male citizens; but we, the whole people, who formed the Union.

Susan B. Anthony

$\mathcal{P}$lant a tree in your garden or a potted plant
in your home and measure its growth
along with your own.

The kiss of the sun for pardon,
The song of the birds for mirth—
One is nearer God's Heart in a garden,
Than anywhere else on earth.

Dorothy Gurney

$\mathcal{B}$e willing to trade security for happiness.
The former is never in your control
and the latter always is.

*I believe that in our constant search for security we
can never gain any peace of mind until we secure
our own soul.*

Margaret Chase Smith

$\mathcal{D}$o things in your own way, without worrying that a man might have done it differently.

The art of being a woman can never consist of being a bad imitation of a man.

Olga Knopf

Stand your ground. Don't back down
from someone bigger or louder than you.

You turn if you want to. This lady's not for turning.

Margaret Thatcher

Watch an hour of public television.

As we look inside the private lives, it's really me and you we're watching on the tube.

Basia

*A*llow yourself to be pampered with a facial, massage, haircut, manicure or back rub.

A fool bolts pleasure, then complains of moral indigestion.

Minna Thomas Antrim
Naked Truth and Veiled Illusions

$\mathcal{R}$eturn to a hobby that you let slide away
because of lack of time for yourself.

*Don't trade the very stuff of your life, time, for
nothing more than dollars. That's a rotten bargain.*

Rita Mae Brown

Sing your favorite song out loud.

Sing, sing a song.
Sing out loud, sing out strong.
Don't worry that it's not good enough
For anyone else to hear.
Just sing, sing a song.

Karen Carpenter

Take a bike ride at the beach, feeling the cool, moist air combine with the warmth of the sun to create a healthy sense of well-being.

Such, thought she, O Sun, art thou! Thy cheering beams pervades the very soul, and drives thence the despondency of cold and darkness.

Jane Porter

ℒaugh from the heart with deep,
bellowing guffaws.

Total absence of humor renders life impossible.

Colette
Chance Acquaintances

Change the one thing about yourself that you've been afraid to because of how others might react.

That's the risk you take if you change: that people you've been involved with won't like the new you. But other people who do will come along.

Lisa Alther

Do something to excess.

Too much of a good thing can be wonderful.

Mae West

$\mathcal{F}$inish that project that's been hanging over your head and feel the relief that accompanies completion.

I went for years without finishing anything. But, of course, when you finish something you can be judged.

Erica Jong

Create your future by envisioning what it looks like, where you are, who you're with and what you're doing.

The most pathetic person in the world is someone who has sight, but has no vision.

Helen Keller

$\mathcal{D}$on't allow anyone to ignore you.
Make yourself someone to be contended with.

We haven't come a long way, we've come a short way. If we hadn't come a short way, no one would be calling us "baby."

Elizabeth Janeway

Stay in bed for an extra half hour
with a good book.

*No matter how big or soft or warm your bed is, you
still have to get out of it.*

Grace Slick

Wrap a small present in beautiful paper and ribbon and give it to yourself.

The more independent you want to be, the more generous you must be with yourself.

Diane Von Furstenberg

Go on an adventure—if only for an hour,
a day or a minute.

*Most any place is Baghdad if you don't know what
will happen in it.*

Edna Ferber
So Big

Begin a journal to record your thoughts, feelings, ideas, hopes and aspirations.

Why do women keep diaries? This form has been an important outlet for women partly because it is an analogue to their lives: emotional, fragmentary, interrupted, modest, not to be taken seriously, private, restricted, daily, trivial, formless, concerned with self, as endless as their tasks.

Mary Jane Moffat

If you don't already have a camera,
buy a disposable one and go out
on a picture-taking expedition.

*The camera makes everyone a tourist in other
people's reality, and eventually in one's own.*

Susan Sontag

$\mathcal{L}$et go of those people who empty your well without a thought of helping to replenish it.

To keep all your old friends is like keeping all your old clothes—pretty soon your closet is so jammed and everything so crushed you can't find anything to wear. Help these friends when they need you; bless the years and happy times when you meant a lot to each other, but try not to have the guilts if new people mean more to you now.

Helen Gurley Brown

$\mathcal{L}$et yourself have a "bad hair day" when
you really need one.

*No woman is all sweetness; even the rose has
thorns.*

Mme. Recamier

$\mathcal{F}$ree yourself from the false confines of time
by leaving your watch at home.

*The clock talked loud. I threw it away, it scared me
what it talked.*

Tillie Olsen
Tell Me a Riddle

Take a walk in the park, taking the time to really see what nature is whispering to you.

Walking is also an ambulation of the mind.

Gretel Ehrlich

$\mathcal{D}$o something that you've been afraid to do
because you don't know exactly what the
outcome will be.

*You gain strength, courage and confidence by
every experience in which you must stop and look
fear in the face . . . You must do the thing that you
think you cannot do.*

Eleanor Roosevelt

Write a poem about your experience
as a woman.

Poetry has a way of teaching one what one needs to know . . . if one is honest.

May Sarton

*H*ave your own film festival in the middle
of the afternoon.

*Does art reflect life? In movies, yes. Because more
than any other art form, films have been a mirror
held up to society's porous face.*

Marjorie Rosen

$\mathcal{E}$at an ice cream cone — triple scoop.

"She should be thinking of higher things."
"Nothing could be higher than food," said Leah.

Ivy Compton-Burnett
The Mighty and Their Fall

*A*nswer only those personal questions
with which you are comfortable,
and pass on those that you're not.

*To frivolous questions silence is ever the best
answer.*

R.M.
Live Within Compasse in Humilitie

ℛun for office or be on a committee
that effects change in a field
that's important to you.

*Women need to see ourselves as individuals capable
of creating change. That is what political and
economic power is all about: having a voice, being
able to shape the future. Women's absence from
decision-making positions has deprived the country
of a necessary perspective.*

Madeleine Kunin

$\mathcal{T}$ake time to enjoy one accomplishment today instead of rushing on to the next task waiting to be done.

$\mathcal{L}$ife isn't a matter of milestones, but of moments.

Rose Kennedy

*H*ave a day free from housework of any kind.

I think housework is the reason most women go to the office.

Heloise

Learn a new word, how airplanes fly,
why bears hibernate for the winter or
what constitutes the mind . . . but learn.

It is the mind that makes the body.

Sojourner Truth

$\mathcal{D}$o something that no one expects
a woman to do—and do it with gusto!

*When she stopped conforming to the conventional
picture of femininity, she finally began to enjoy
being a woman.*

Betty Friedan

$\mathcal{L}$ook at the lines in your face as an intricate
fabric woven from your life's experiences —
both good and bad — but always yours alone.

*It matters more what's in a woman's face than
what's on it.*

Claudette Colbert

Read today's paper from beginning to end,
giving yourself permission to pass over
those parts in which you have no interest.

*Dead news like dead love has no phoenix in its
ashes.*

Enid Bagnold
National Velvet

Call an old friend and reminisce about good times that you've shared.

In my friend, I find a second self.

Isabel Norton

$\mathcal{B}$e less ready to compromise and more willing
to go to battle for what you believe in.

*The lazy pattern of living had reinstated itself, had
returned an assuagement made of compromise
and complacency. It had made things safe again
between them.*

Octavia Waldo
Roman Spring

120

Walk barefoot in the grass on a spring day.

The air and the earth interpenetrated in the warm gusts of spring . . . The air one breathed was saturated with earthy smells and the grass under foot had a reflection of blue sky in it.

Willa Cather
Death Comes for the Archbishop

$\mathcal{F}$ree yourself from unnecessary stress
with the knowledge that it is not your
responsibility to solve anyone else's problem.

The true secret of giving advice is, after you honestly have given it, to be perfectly indifferent to whether it is taken or not, and never persist in trying to set people right.

Hannah Whitall Smith

Allow yourself to think about that person
you've been trying to erase from the landscape
of your life and remember with fondness
the good times shared.

Little trails through my heart that are
Still warm—my remembrances of you.

Erinna

*A*sk for help instead of struggling
to do it all yourself.

*It was usual for the women to do their own plant-
ing, but if a woman was sick or for some reason
unable to attend to her planting she sometimes
cooked a feast, to which she invited the members of
her age society, and asked them to plant her field for
her.*

Buffalo Bird Woman

124

*H*old a baby and rejoice in the knowledge
that miracles are real.

*Miracles are natural. When they do not occur,
something has gone wrong.*

Helen Schucman
A Course in Miracles

Give your honest opinion without fearing
that someone else's might be different—
because it probably will.

Beautiful faces are those that wear
Whole-souled honesty printed there.

Ellen Palmer Allerton
Beautiful Things

Wear something that you've always wanted to wear but didn't because of a fear of what other people might think.

When I am an old woman I shall wear purple
With a red hat which doesn't go, and doesn't suit
*   me....*
And pick flowers in other people's gardens
And learn to spit....
But maybe I ought to practise a little now?
So people who know me are not too shocked and
*   surprised*
When suddenly I am old, and start to wear purple.

Jenny Joseph
Warning

Go without makeup and feel how clean
your soul feels when not encumbered
by the trappings of a society that wants you
to look like everyone else.

*The most frequent form of doubt assumed [by a
woman] is the conviction that [she] is ugly . . . this
conviction is quite independent of whatever the actu-
al facts may be.*

Karen Horney
Feminine Psychology

Take the afternoon off and do something you've been wanting to do for a long time but thought was too frivolous.

If you really want something you can figure out how to make it happen.

Cher

$\mathcal{T}$ell a joke . . . and be the first to laugh.

If my heart were not light, I would die.

Joanna Baillie

*A*sk for what you want without an apology
or explanation.

*I'm tough, I'm ambitious, and I know exactly what
I want. If that makes me a bitch, okay.*

Madonna

Be who you are, rather than who others
expect you to be.

*In my early days I was a sepia Hedy Lamarr. Now
I'm black and a woman, singing my own way.*

Lena Horne

𝒦indle your spirit by no longer associating with people who would like to see it extinguished.

𝒴ou can't kill the spirit. It's like a mountain old and strong; it lives on and on.

Naomi Littlebear
Like a Mountain

Do not stoically shoulder the blame
for something you did not do.

*In passing, also, I would like to say that the first
time Adam had a chance he laid the blame on a
woman.*

Nancy Astor

Tell yourself the one thing you wish you'd heard from your father but never did—and believe it.

I wanted him to cherish and approve of me, not as he had when I was a child, but as the woman I was, who had her own mind and had made her own choices.

Adrienne Rich
Blood, Bread and Poetry

135

$\mathcal{F}$orgive someone for a long past transgression and be free from the chains of resentment.

You can't be fueled by bitterness. It can eat you up, but it cannot drive you.

Benazir Bhutto
Daughter of Destiny

Think and say positive self-messages
about your body rather than verbally
abusing yourself.

The obsession of slenderness might well be considered one of the most serious forms of suffering affecting women in America today.

Kim Chernin
The Obsession

Spend an hour with someone you care about instead of with someone who needs you.

My days ran away so fast. I simply ran after my days.

Leah Morton
I Am a Woman — & a Jew

Spend a weekend without plans
made in advance.

*Life is what happens to you while you're making
other plans.*

Betty Talmadge

*A*sk for, and expect to get, the raise that you deserve.

Women have been so brainwashed by the destructive female culture that taught them to associate money with sin, evil and everything crude ... that it would take an entire book to entangle the subconscious fears and incredible fantasies that the simple noun "money" evokes in most women.

Betty Lehan Harragan
Games Mother Never Taught You

Correct people when they improperly call you, or other women, chair*man*, mail*man*, fire*man* or any other word that ends in *man* — because you are not.

This monopoly over language is one of the means by which males have ensured their own primacy, and consequently have ensured the invisibility or "other" nature of females.

Dale Spender
Man Made Language

Tape over the voice inside your head that says "I can't" with one that says "I will."

I can therefore I am.

Simone Weil

Create a balance between work and play
so that you'll be able to give your best to both.

*You know, your career is just your career. Your life
is your life!*

Sissy Spacek

*I*nstead of asking for permission, just do it. Only children must ask permission.

Be bold. If you're going to make an error, make it a doozy, and don't be afraid to hit the ball.

Billie Jean King

$\mathcal{L}$et people know when they've hurt you
so that you can heal sooner.

*$\mathcal{L}$ife appears to me too short to be spent in nursing
animosity or registering wrong.*

Charlotte Brontë

*F*ocus on changing the things that are in
the domain of your control and let go
of those that aren't.

In this short Life
That only lasts an hour
How much—how little—is
Within our power.

Emily Dickinson

At every fork in the road,
consciously choose happiness.

You don't get to choose how you're going to die. Or when. You can decide how you're going to live now.

Joan Baez

Sit for a half hour in the afternoon sun
of an early fall day, saying good-bye
to the final rays of summer.

The sun lay like a friendly arm across her shoulder.

Margorie Kinnan Rawlings
South Moon Under

Let go of the fear, the shoulds and the oughts, and do that one thing that you've been wanting to do your whole life long.

Many older women are inhibited and afraid to act. It is such a waste of human potential.

Frances Lear

$\mathcal{A}$sk for emotional support when you need it instead of bearing the burden yourself.

We are all held in place by the pressure of the crowd around us. We must all lean upon others. Let us see that we lean gracefully and freely and acknowledge the support.

Margaret Collier Graham
Gifts and Givers

$\mathcal{A}$llow yourself to love — whether to love the day, a man, a woman or a flower — but love.

Love is the only thing that we can carry with us when we go, and it makes the end so easy.

Louisa May Alcott

$\mathcal{B}$e spontaneous—do something without
planning, thinking or worrying
how it will turn out.

Why not seize the pleasure at once? How often is happiness destroyed by preparation, foolish preparation!

Jane Austen

Play to your fullest capacity instead of holding back for fear of breaking the rules.

All of my life I've been competing and competing to win.

Babe Didrikson Zaharias

$\mathcal{L}$et go of trying to control everyone and
everything around you and experience
the release that comes from abandoning
the impossible.

*Trying to be God has an additional effect: it over-
stresses the human organism and eventually leads
to death. I firmly believe our lives could be relatively
stress-free if we relinquished our illusion of control.*

Anne Wilson Schaef
When Society Becomes An Addict

*H*ave a long talk with the person or thing
that you fear the most and emerge victorious
simply for having done so.

*If you banish fear, nothing terribly bad can happen
to you.*

Margaret Bourke-White

Make a decision without asking for anyone's opinion.

Think wrongly, if you please, but in all cases think for yourself.

Doris Lessing

Don't smile unless you really think it's funny.

All humans smile when they're happy. But women often smile when they feel vulnerable. . . .Actually, smiling is frequently associated with subordinate status. This may be an inborn trait.

Dr. Pat Heim
Hardball for Women

*A*pologize only when you've made
an outrageous mistake, not because
someone made you feel stupid.

*By refusing to assume responsibility for other peo-
ple's mistakes, we not only cause them to assume
responsibility for themselves, but we take back control of our lives. We move out of the victim role and
into the role of responsible adult.*

Dr. Lois P. Frankel
Women, Anger and Depression

Call your doctor by his or her first name,
particularly when you are called by yours.

*One-way first name calling always means in
equality—witness servants, children and dogs.*

Marjorie Karmel

$\mathcal{D}$ecide consciously what you want to do rather than taking the path of least resistance.

We are swallowed up only when we are willing for it to happen.

Nathalie Sarraute

$\mathcal{T}$urn an apparent failure into
a valuable learning experience.

If you have made mistakes, even serious ones, there is always another chance for you. What we call failure is not the falling down, but the staying down.

Mary Pickford

Say it over and over until your voice is heard.

Can we be like drops of water falling on the stone?
Splashing, breaking, dispersing in air.
Weaker than the stone by far,
But be aware that as time goes by
The rock will wear away.
And the water comes again.

Meg Christian

When you turn out the lights tonight rest well with the knowledge that who you are is truly enough—you need not be anything more.

I seldom think about my limitations, and they never make me sad. Perhaps there is just a touch of yearning at times; but it is vague, like a breeze among flowers.

Helen Keller

ABOUT THE AUTHOR

Dr. Lois P. Frankel, a partner in The Frankel & Fox Group, Consultants in Employee Development, has nearly twenty years experience in the field of human resources development. She travels internationally to consult with organizations of all sizes to help them meet their objectives by maximizing the development of individuals and teams. With particular expertise in designing and facilitating training programs related to team building, the empowerment of women and leadership development, Dr. Frankel also coaches individuals to avoid career derailment.

Her diverse list of clients includes Baskin-Robbins, the County of Los Angeles, ARCO, Siemens Solar Industries, AlliedSignal Aerospace, Nissan, RKO General, AMGEN, the Los Angeles Regional Food Bank, Atlantic Richfield Indonesia, Clinicas Del Camino Real, Gay and Lesbian Community Services Center and Los Angeles Women's Foundation. In addition to her fee clients, Dr. Frankel also provides pro bono consultation and workshops to community agencies.

Dr. Frankel has appeared on talk radio and television programs, at association conferences and at corporate workshops and retreats. Her employment-related journal articles include "Depressed Organizations: Identifying Symptoms and Overcoming Causes"; "Employee Coaching: The Way to Gain Commitment, Not Just Compliance"; and the soon-to-be-published "De-Railment: How the Past Prevents Future Success." In addition to *Kindling the Spirit: Acts of Kindness and Words of Courage for Women*, she is the author of *Women, Anger and Depression: Strategies for Self-Empowerment*, also published by Health Communications, Inc.

A member of the American Society for Training and Development, the American Psychological Association and the National Association of Women Business Owners, Dr. Frankel formerly had a private practice of psychotherapy and is a licensed psychotherapist. She holds a doctorate in Counseling Psychology from the University of Southern California, a Master's degree in Counseling and a Bachelor's degree in Psychology. She enjoys residing in La Canada, California where she can play tennis, bicycle, hike and perseverate over her golf game year-round.

Should you be interested in contacting Dr. Frankel to consult with your organization, speak at a convention, or conduct a workshop or retreat, she can be reached in writing at The Frankel & Fox Group, 445 South Figueroa Street, Suite 2700, Los Angeles, California 90071 or by phone at 213-624-5716.